40 Days of Spiritual Crumbs

Katherine L. Harvell

Diligence Publishing Company
Bloomfield, New Jersey

The Scriptures in this book are from the King James Version, The New International Version, The NSRV, Amplified and/or other versions of the Bible.

40 Days of Spiritual Crumbs

To contact Katherine L. Harvell to preach or speak at your church, organization, seminar or conference email: harvellk326@yahoo.com

40 Days of Spiritual Crumbs

ISBN: 978-1-7331353-6-8

Printed in the United States

40 Days of Spiritual Crumbs

Katherine L. Harvell

TABLE OF CONTENTS

Truth Lord: yet the dogs eat the crumbs which fall from their master's table."

Matthew 15:27

FOREWORD

⁙ ⁙ ⁙

I was truly blessed when Minister Katherine Harvell asked me to write the foreword for her book, *"40 Days of Spiritual Crumbs."* I have known Katherine for many years, as we attended the same church for over a decade.

I met Kathrine as she served as a greeter at The Cathedral International in Perth Amboy. I have fond memories of the many Sundays after church spent talking with Katherine. We would stand in the lobby and talk for what seemed like hours about her writing and the books that she wanted to write. She even shared some of her inspirational writings with me at that time. The same writings turned into booklets for her ministry team. Back then, I thought her writings were powerful. Today, after reading this book, I can say the same.

As I read through *"40 Days of Spiritual Crumbs,"* I was encouraged, uplifted, and inspired to keep moving forward and to keep holding on to the LORD's unchanging hand. I felt the anointing of the Spirit of God as I read through the devotional for each day. There were some personal challenges in my life that I had to go through while reading this book, but this book helped to pull me through.

I am confident that everyone who reads this book will be empowered. There is strength to be found within the pages of the book that you are holding in your hands.

It's as if Katherine has put her ear to the mouth of God and prophetically written what she heard. You will hear from God and feel the presence of God as you delve into the pages of this book. Drink deeply of the fresh waters and eat of the crumbs of the spiritual bread that has been released through the heart and pen of Katherine L. Harvell. You will be refreshed, and your soul will be nourished and replenished. I hear the Lord saying, "Well done on this assignment, Katherine. Well done!"

Pastor Rebecca Simmons
New Creation Christian Ministries
Hillside, New Jersey

—————— ✢ ✢ ✢ ——————

4O DAYS OF
SPIRITUAL CRUMBS

—————— ✢ ✢ ✢ ——————

INTRODUCTION

40 Days of Spiritual Crumbs

This is the revised publication of *"40 Days of Spiritual Crumbs."* I will begin by saying my life has been changed forever by some of the words you are about to read on the following pages. I've written from my own journey through pain and healing. Deliverance has come to my house. Hallelujah!

God has been with me every step of the way. I realized God still loves me, no matter how disobedient I might have been. He is and always will be a loving and forgiving God.

I stayed away from church almost twenty years before joining Mount Olive in Hackensack, New Jersey. In 2000, we moved, and I joined Cathedral International Church in Perth Amboy, New Jersey. I soon became involved in several ministries. As president of the hospitality ministry, I began sending out monthly newsletters. The newsletters consisted of a corporate prayer with Scriptures. Friends, some in person and others by mail, told me they were blessed to receive a prayer. Later in the year, the Lord gave me the book title *"40 Days of Spiritual Crumbs."*

One day during prayer and fasting, I began reading Matthew, Chapter 15:22-28. The verses talk about the Canaanite woman who came to Jesus, asking help for her daughter who was vexed with a demon. The woman said to Jesus, "Even the dogs eat the crumbs which fall from the master's table."

Her faith prompted Jesus to bless her daughter immediately. The mother was healed also from her own worry and pain. I'm sure she experienced many sleepless nights before coming in contact with Jesus. She was determined to get a breakthrough for her child. She was tired of going through the same thing over and over getting no results. After crying out to God in desperation for healing, she received a crumb blessing!

When we're desperate, we take desperate measures to receive peace. Like most of us, this Canaanite woman needed peace in her home and peace in her mind. She knew Jesus was the only one who could give her real peace. Jesus just happened to be passing through her city. We all know that nothing just happens; it is the will and plan of God. Somehow, this mother had to get to Jesus. At that moment, she took a chance and her faith was backed by action. Strong faith never allowed doubt to cloud her mind. She believed Jesus could and would perform a miracle for her. Jesus could not neglect her cry for help. She didn't care what others thought or said. Like some mothers today, she had a nagging problem that needed immediate attention.

In Christ Jesus, we find rest and answers to our prayers. We come into His presence to feast on the blessings He drops for us. This woman's humility made her glad to receive the crumbs. Those around tried to send her away, but she refused to give up. She was determined to get her miracle. We have to stay in the face of God until we get His attention. Just like this Canaanite woman, many around us may say or think we are not worthy of God's love.

We have been made joint heirs with Christ. We are loved with an everlasting love. This woman kept crying after Jesus until He responded to her need. Although the daughter was not physically present at the time, she did receive healing. We understand there is no distance in prayer. I know my late mother prayed many prayers for me. I once lost my way, but her unwavering prayers stopped Satan from destroying my life. The prayers of a mother are powerful. This Canaanite mother was crying out to Jesus for her child's healing. How many today are crying out for our children, grandchildren and great grandchildren? Do we have faith and are we praying for the children of this world? How many are praying for the parents? Is anyone praying for marriages and families? Whatever our children and loved ones are going through, we cannot sit idly by. We will stand in the gap, interceding, exercising our faith, and expecting answers to our petitions.

Faith is wisdom, humility, meekness, patience and perseverance in prayer. Personally speaking, I've been healed by some of the crumbs dropped from the Master's table, and I'm sharing them with anyone who is hungry for healing and restoration. God wants us to live whole and productive lives while here on earth. If life has ever seemed unfair, left you feeling neglected and unloved, then you've just picked up the perfect tool to help peel away years of pain and self-sabotage. This healing book/journal has been prayerfully released. It is time to forgive and receive freedom from those who may have hurt us in the past. Unfortunately, many have been sexually, physically, or emotionally abused. Some may be going through these horrible situations right now, but God is able to heal and set free in the name of Jesus. God will deliver while providing a way of escape from past hurt and pain.

This book is written to help us along our healing journey. Change and deliverance will come as we step into the pages, pray, sit for a season and ask God to direct our lives. As you begin to read and go through this healing tunnel of orchestrated love, allow the Lord to minister to every need.

God's desire is that we live victoriously and without old pain, doubt, fear, and stress. We can unpack old baggage, let go of bitterness and move into our divine purpose. It is amazing to see what God can do through us as we let go and trust Him completely. Our cares are placed in His hands. Our burdens fall at His feet. We pick up the crumbs that fall from the Master's table. Our Master is Jesus. I pray for many divine healings to take place. God will be greatly exalted. I prophesy in the name of Jesus, that family members will be rejoined together in love and forgiveness. This book is meant to lead someone, who feels they've been in the desert far too long, to the healing waters of Jesus. Drink deeply, and let the Scriptures and prayers quench the parched areas of life.

The prayers and meditations have come to release a pathway, to break yokes, and release healing to the mind. Allow the Holy Spirit to minister in a fresh new way, as He heals the hidden areas. I pray for divine healing as we reflect and write out our own thoughts and prayers. I pray this book will bless children, men and women all over the world. This is a book of prophetic utterances written by the leading of the Holy Spirit. There are words that have no beginning and no ending; they only exist in God. As we feast in the Word of God, He will begin to give revelation. I believe God is doing something supernatural in the lives of His people. Use this book as a daily prayer guide. Delve into the Scriptures and see how God is speaking to our thoughts, desires, and aspirations. Write about areas needing God's healing and restoration. Jot down whatever comes to mind during the next forty days. Use a journal or plain paper if more space is needed. It would help if we write a letter to God, a letter of forgiveness to ourselves, or to someone else. There are personal areas in our lives that only God can heal. Some memories are too painful to be verbally spoken. Write the incident down and burn it, thus releasing it to God.

Spend some one on one time in fellowship with the Lord. Allow Him time to speak, while listening attentively to hear answers. Turn off all distractions, TV, cell phones, electronics and tune into God. Turn off gossiping and stop judging people. Ask God to give you friends who will pray with and for you and follow up to see how you're doing without telling everyone your business. Spend more time speaking the desired outcome to God instead of repeating the problem.

We all have experienced frustration, rejection, opposition and failure. When we ask, knock, and seek the will of God for our lives, there is peace, joy, and love. Therefore, we will live victorious lives through Jesus Christ. My sincere prayer is that after journeying through *"40 Days of Spiritual Crumbs"* God will heal you completely in every area... So, arise and be healed!

Katherine L. Harvell

DAY 1

❖ ❖ ❖

Somebody Ought To Testify

"Thy testimonies also are my delight and my counsellors." Psalm 119:24

My personal testimony: A believer's life and word serve as testimony to the world. We all have much to testify about. I was baptized at the age of five. At age six, I spoke in tongues, but I didn't understand the gift or the Giver. Dad drove Mom and I to church two or three times a week. I remember during every service there were testimonies. I loved to hear the elders tell of God's goodness. It was fun and exciting until I started getting teased and called names at school.

Our strict religion taught us ways to look different; wear long dresses, no pants or shorts, no earrings, no lipstick, no dancing, no prom, and many other restrictions. I endured ridicule because of my religious beliefs. During my teenage years, I grew more isolated and resentful. I turned away from church and God. I became rebellious and angry because of peer pressures. I mentally planned to leave home and never return to organized religion. I ventured out to experience what the world had to offer. I found out the hard way that turning my back was not a good decision. I was blessed with a praying mother who never gave up on me.

Some twenty years later, I returned to the church. I came to realize God was with me all the time. He protected me through the prayers of my mother. Before my second marriage, there were times I had no food on the table. I sought shelter from family, which kept my child and I from being homeless. I was wounded and bitter. God's never-ending love embraced me all along. He protected and guided me by His grace and mercy. God let me know it's never too late to return to Him and ask forgiveness. We all have unique testimonies, stories only we can tell. That's how God planned it. I am so thankful He turned my life back around.

Which testimonies can you and I share with someone who is hurting, suicidal, troubled, going through a broken relationship or involved in a life of sin and confusion? We all have a voice to witness for Christ. Our stories have power. Our testimonies will help free others from bondage.

Prayer For Today: Lord please reveal when and how I should tell others about the struggles you brought me through. Let me not be ashamed to share the details of my story with others. I pray lives are transformed for the better through my testimonies. Lord break curses, yokes, and bondage. Reveal yourself and let your glory shine forth. In Jesus name, Amen.

Somebody Ought To Testify (Day 1)

Scriptures: Jeremiah 29:11, Ezekiel 16:60, Philippians 1:6

_____

_____

_____

_____

_____

_____

_____

_____

_____

_____

_____

_____

_____ ❖ ❖ ❖ _____

—————————— ❖ ❖ ❖ ——————————

*"We all have a voice to witness for
Christ. Our stories have power.
Our testimonies will help free
others from bondage."*

—————————— ❖ ❖ ❖ ——————————

DAY 2

❖ ❖ ❖

Take The Limits Off God

Now unto Him that is able to do exceedingly abundantly above all that we ask or think, according to the power that works in us.
Ephesians 3:20

Although we can believe God for the little things, we must begin to completely trust Him in every situation. God is larger than any imaginable obstacle. He is still healing individuals from cancer, AIDS, depression, high blood pressure, kidney disorders, lung, heart, liver and other diseases. He is still increasing incomes, giving new homes and cars, putting children through college and keeping us from dangers seen and unseen. With Christ, all things are possible. We serve a God who stepped out on nothing and said, "Let there be." Let God be whatever we need Him to be. He is not a God who can be boxed in.

Situations change as we make positive declarations about ourselves and God. It is our faith that moves Him. It's time to stop telling God what we cannot do. Words of affirmation make our lives better. Let's begin to encourage ourselves by making positive statements such as, "I'm smart enough," "I have background know-ledge," "I have money for supplies," "My age is not a problem," and other uplifting phrases. Get ready to take the limits off God and follow Him wholeheartedly!

Prayer For Today: I desire to believe and trust in God. I put my complete trust in the God given abilities. Help me remember and believe in you God to bring me through every trial and circumstance. I can do all things through Christ who strengthens me. There are no limits to what can happen when I take the limits off. The joy of the Lord is my strength. In Jesus name I pray, Amen.

Take The Limits Off God (Day 2)

Scriptures: Exodus 4:10, Job 42:1-2, Matthew 17:19-20

_____

_____

_____

_____

_____

_____

_____

_____

_____

_____

_____

❖ ❖ ❖

DAY 3

⁘ ⁘ ⁘

I'm About My Father's Business

And He said to them, How is it you had to look for Me? Did you not see and know that it is necessary for Me to be in My Father's house and about My Father's business? Luke 2:49-50 (Amplified Bible)

God has called each of us to be about His business. We are to reach, teach, and preach. God wants to use us for His Kingdom purposes. He has called us to speak words of love and share His love with our neighbors. God called us to minister and serve the broken, sick, needy, and hungry. Are we about our Father's business? Are we telling others about giving their lives to Jesus and having a relationship with the Savior?

We love while serving and helping others. If we are doorkeepers, we want to be the best at making everyone welcome. If we are missionaries, deacons, trustees, elders, ministers, or worship leaders, we want to do our best for the Lord. Even on our jobs, in schools, hospitals, our homes, and wherever we are, we strive to give our best service. God does not want to hear, "I didn't do it because I don't have a title, my sister or brother didn't help me, and no one else bothered to help, so I didn't go either." God is more concerned about what we do as individuals. Therefore, the question will always be, "What am I doing to make life different and better for someone else?" God has put words in our mouths. Our desire is to be used for His glory. We want to hear, "Well done my, good and faithful servant."

Prayer For Today: Lord God please order my steps. Enable me to hear your directions and follow your divine will. I surrender my all to you as I reach out to help others. Have your way in my life. In Jesus name I pray, Amen.

I'm About My Father's Business (Day 3)

Scriptures: Luke 2:49-50, Jeremiah 1:5-7

_____

_____

_____

_____

_____

_____

_____

_____

_____

_____

_____

_____

———————— ✤ ✤ ✤ ————————

DAY 4

❖ ❖ ❖

Surrender, Let Go and Let God

**Casting the whole of your care [all your
anxieties, all your worries, all your
concerns, once and for all] on Him, for He
cares for you affectionately and
cares about you watchfully.
1 Peter 5:7 (Amplified Bible)**

The word surrender means to give up claim to, also to give over or yield voluntarily. Are we holding on to old pain, disappointments from former relationships, regrets, and anger? Oftentimes, we have attempted to bury these and other emotions. We believe if we push them down deep enough, we won't have to deal with them anymore. Everything not mentally and properly processed has a way of resurfacing in our lives. Pray, surrender all to God and be delivered. He is the only yoke destroying burden bearer.

Real strength is knowing when to let go and let God. We surrender old habits of impulsive shopping, foul language, sensitive ego, jealously, need to always be right, need to always have it together, judging others, anger, and revenge. God help us surrender everything negative about life that keeps us from having a sincere relationship with you. Without God, we settle for merely existing, stumbling through life and missing all the promised blessings.

Prayer For Today: Lord I surrender myself to you. Take complete control of every area of my life. I refuse to worry or be discouraged. Come Holy Spirit and minister to me. God help me to let go of anger, hurt, and disappointments. I pray for my enemies. I surrender my thoughts, dreams, possessions, hopes and aspirations. God please keep me humble and totally surrendered to you. I pray in Jesus name, Amen.

Surrender, Let Go and Let God (Day 4)

Scripture: 2 Corinthians 12:9

--- ⁕ ⁕ ⁕ ---

DAY 5

— ❖ ❖ ❖ —

Make A Decision

Multitudes, multitudes in the valley of decision! For the day of the Lord is near in the valley of decision. Joel 3:14 (NKJV)

Along with the closing of each calendar year, we realize there are seasons in our lives that need to close as well. Many habits routinely take first priority and keep us from walking closer to God. We are clueless concerning behaviors which destroy us and keep us from receiving God's best. The same New Year's resolutions are made year after year. After a couple of weeks, we have gone back to our same old ways. This time, we vow to make better decisions and stick with them. Make a decision to let the pain of the past go. Make a decision to love in spite of all we have gone through. Decide to be free in mind and spirit by removing the things that are detrimental to our well-being.

Esther made a decision to fast and pray for her people. Job made a decision to trust God against all odds. Ruth made a decision to follow Naomi and her God. David made a decision to follow hard after God, even after he had sinned. Shadrach, Meshach, and Abednego made a decision not to bow down to false gods or golden images of King Nebuchadnezzar. Hannah made a decision to pray to God. In essence, make a decision daily to do what pleases God.

Prayer For Today: Lord God please give me clear vision and a sound mind to make the right decisions. I pray my thoughts and actions line up with my life's purpose. Keep me from wavering and giving up too soon. God please help me make decisions that flow with your will. In Jesus name I pray, Amen.

Make A Decision (Day 5)

Scriptures: James 1:5, Proverbs 16:9, Isaiah 30:21

_____

_____

_____

_____

_____

_____

_____

_____

_____

_____

_____

_____

_____

⋅⋮⋅ ⋅⋮⋅ ⋅⋮⋅

DAY 6

❖ ❖ ❖

God Said, "Worship Me"

But the hour is coming, and now is, when true worshippers will worship the Father in spirit and truth; for the Father is seeking such to worship Him. John 4:23 (NKJV)

Worship means to adore, obey, reverence and to focus positive attention on God. Any action or attitude that expresses praise, love, and appreciation for God is considered worship. Worship is expressed through obedience, the way we give and how we treat others. Worship can be private or public. There is a level of faith in worship that cannot be explained. When we worship God, we are letting Him know how much we love and trust Him.

While I was praying a few days ago, God said to me, "Worship Me. Stop asking for things, and just worship Me. I know what you need before you ask. Begin to thank Me in advance for what I am about to do. I am getting ready to pour out many blessings. Pray for others and just WORSHIP ME. WORSHIP ME. WORSHIP ME."

God is a Spirit. His worshippers must worship Him in Spirit and truth.

Prayer For Today: Lord I thank you. I worship you for who you are. I acknowledge your great love. You know my needs and what's best for me. I worship you, I adore you and bless your name. God please continue to shower me with your love and mercy. I worship you in beauty and holiness. I worship you in Spirit and truth. I give you all glory, honor, and praise. God keep me close to you. In the name of Jesus I pray, Amen.

God Said, "Worship Me" (Day 6)

Scriptures: Exodus 34:8, 14, Psalm 29:2, Psalm 95:6-7, Psalm 96:9, John 4:24

_____

_____

_____

_____

_____

_____

_____

_____

_____

_____

_____

_____

_____

⁜ ⁜ ⁜

DAY 7

Don't Be Crippled By Memories

Brethren, I count not myself to have apprehended: but this one thing I do, forgetting those things which are behind, and reaching forth unto those things which are before. I press toward the mark for the prize of the high calling of God in Christ Jesus. Philippians 3:13-14 (KJV)

The Apostle Paul had reason to feel sorry about his past. He held the coats and watched as Stephen, the first Christian martyr, was stoned. Most of us have wrestled with shame and guilt because of life experiences at some point and time. Some of us are haunted by nightmares and traumatic events of which we had no control.

We have found ourselves in situations and asked ourselves, "How did I get involved in this?"

The things we were surrounded by, clubs we belonged to, places we frequented, and people we were involved with caused crippling effects. Memories of old habits keep blocking us from attempting our dreams and fulfilling our purpose. We can also become lame and incapable of doing the things God has assigned for us since the beginning of time. We are stuck and cannot move forward because of past events. Day by day our future is passing, while we live in yesterday. Truth is, we cannot go back and change or undo what was done to us. How do we stand and pick up the bed of self-pity, self-hatred, and other self-inflicted bondage?

First, we repent, ask forgiveness for ourselves and anyone who may have caused us harm. We pray, asking God to heal our minds as we release all the pain from the past to Him. We then arm ourselves with the Word of God to resist Satan's attack on our past and future. Lastly, we step out of the old and refuse to be crippled by memories. It may take some time and effort, but in Christ all things are possible. The past is over. All things have been made new.

Prayer For Today: Lord God help me forgive and forget those things that are behind me. Heal me from haunting debilitating memories that serve no purpose. Help me live each day in total surrender to you God. Please heal my mind and my heart. Remind me of your love and tender mercies that are new every morning. In Jesus name I pray, Amen.

Don't Be Crippled By Memories (Day 7)

Scriptures: Romans 8:1, 1 John 1:9

_____

_____

_____

_____

_____

_____

_____

_____

_____

_____

_____

_____

_____

_____

_____

_____

_____

_____

_____

——————————— ✤ ✤ ✤ ———————————

— ❖ ❖ ❖ —

"Lord God help me forgive and forget
those things that are behind me.
Heal me from haunting debilitating
memories that serve no purpose."

— ❖ ❖ ❖ —

DAY 8

———— ⁜ ⁜ ⁜ ————

All Things New

***And he that sat upon the throne said,
Behold I make all things new. And he said
unto me, Write: for these words are true and
faithful. Revelation 21:5 (KJV)***

How often do we hold on to our own
preconceived ideas, assumptions, false
statements and old wives' tales? We hang on to
names and labels other people have attached to
us. Too often we believe these untruths. But
seriously speaking, what does God's Word say
about us? God has called us beloved sons and
daughters. He loves us so much that He sent His
only begotten Son to reconcile us back to Himself.
When we become Christians, we are made brand
new, (2 Corinthians 5:17).

Being made new in Christ; we drop old habits
and forget how to play the same old games.
Through Christ, we learn to treat people with love
and respect. We are not so quick to judge and find
fault in others. We work out our own soul
salvation, while showing others the way to Christ.
God said, "Write, for these words are true and
faithful." We can take God at His Word because
He is not a man that should lie. God's Word will
not, cannot return unto Him void. It shall

accomplish that which it is sent to do. He is doing a new thing in us, with us, and even in spite of us. To God be all the glory!

Prayer For Today: Lord I thank you for the new things you are already doing in my life. Please continue to prepare me for each new blessing. Mold me, heal me, structure my thoughts and shape my ideas. Help me to walk out your prepared purpose and plan for my life. Bless my life, my family and friends. Thank you for the new promises. In Jesus name I pray, Amen.

All Things New (Day 8)

Scriptures: Isaiah 42:9, Jeremiah 1:5

DAY 9

‡ ‡ ‡

Believe

**So, you see, it is impossible to please God
without faith. Anyone who wants to come to
him must believe that there is a God and
that he rewards those who sincerely seek
him. Hebrews 11:6 (NLT)**

The Word of God offers us promises of a
fulfilling and eternal life. Whosoever believes
will have life and live more abundantly. If we
believe, we will keep His commandments and not
only be hearers of His Word, but doers as well.
Believers become more effective witnesses by
allowing God to operate freely. Today, share God's
love with someone who may be struggling. Hold
others up in prayer and believe God for their
healing and deliverance. Only God is capable of
doing what seems impossible.

Through a life of consistent prayer and Bible
reading, we can believe and experience Jesus for
ourselves. We can believe Him to free us from
debt, depression, pain, isolation, abuse and
addictions. Yes, I believe God is turning defeat
into victory. He is turning negative situations
around in our homes, in our children, our work
and ministries. God is turning sickness into
wellness, poverty into wealth, and sadness into

joy. God has a way of aligning our belief with His will for our lives. I am expecting God to do mighty and marvelous things among us.... because I believe.

Prayer For Today: God I believe your Word. Reveal yourself to me even the more. Take charge of my thoughts. Help me in my desire to trust you completely. I believe the Holy Spirit. In you God, I live, move, and have my being. In the mighty name of Jesus I pray, Amen.

Believe (Day 9)

Scriptures: Proverbs 3:5, Mark 10:27, John 6:29, John 14:1

_____

_____

_____

_____

_____

_____

_____

_____

_____

_____

_____

_____

_____

❖ ❖ ❖

DAY 10

———— ✜ ✜ ✜ ————

Count Your Many Blessings

**You will experience all these blessings if you
obey the Lord your God: you will be blessed
in the towns and in the country.
Deuteronomy 28:2-3 (NLT)**

How often do we complain about what is not going right in our lives? We love to ask God questions like, "Why do bad things always happen to me?" or "Why did my loved one have to leave me?" Sometimes we don't realize how much we grumble and complain. Do we ever stop to count our blessings? Are we ever grateful for what we already have? Let us not compare our blessings with the blessings of others. We may not have all or be able to do the things we desire, yet God has given each of us something unique. We cannot change yesterday, but we can give thanks for blessings hidden in events we thought were mistakes. Calm down and take time to count the many blessings we enjoy daily. Look around and take inventory of life. We realize our good days really do outweigh our bad days. Although there seems to be a lot going wrong, thank God for all the good things taking place. Hallelujah! Relax. Enjoy each day of life. Celebrate all the blessings from God.

Prayer For Today: Lord I give thanks that your hand of protection is upon me. You keep me from all evil. You are my deliverer, my healer and protector. Cover me with your grace. Hide me in the cleft of your mercy. Bless my going out and coming in. Seal me in your Holy Spirit. Lord I am forever grateful for my many blessings. I continue to believe. In Jesus name I pray, Amen.

Count Your Many Blessings (Day 10)

Scriptures: Deuteronomy 28:11-12, 1 Chronicles: 4:10

_____
_____
_____
_____
_____
_____
_____
_____
_____
_____
_____
_____
_____

⊹ ⊹ ⊹

DAY 11

❖ ❖ ❖

Doing God's Will

***Now the God of peace, that brought again
from the dead our Lord Jesus, that great
shepherd of the sheep, through the blood of
the everlasting covenant, make you perfect
in every good work to do his will, working in
you that which is well pleasing in his sight
through Jesus Christ; to whom be glory
forever and forever, Amen.***
Hebrews 12:20-21

What keeps us from doing God's will? Is it work, family, business, school, or being in wrong relationships? Disorder and chaos are some of the things that disconnect us from our purpose. We get very busy with our daily affairs. We fail to get still long enough to hear God. We have all been called to serve, and the Holy Spirit guides us to the center of His will. God instructs us to do certain things, but we pay no attention to Him. While trying to hide or go in the opposite direction like Jonah, we ignore His voice. Our pride and ego take control. In other words, we say 'no' to God.

If it is the will of God, we must be obedient and do it to the best of our ability. It may hurt our flesh, but it's God's desire to correct something in our lives. He wants to strengthen us for current and future tasks. After all is said and done, the outcome will reveal it was the will of God concerning us. Finally, it is about God's divine will being done.

Prayer For Today: Lord it is in you, for you, and because of you that I desire to walk upright. Please lead and guide me in your pure, perfect, and holy will. Give me wisdom and insight to understand your ways. It is my desire to cooperate in doing the perfect will of God. Order my steps in your Word. In Jesus name I pray, Amen.

Doing God's Will (Day 11)

Scripture: Psalm 37:23

_____

_____

_____

_____

_____

_____

_____

_____

_____

_____

_____

✢ ✢ ✢

DAY 12

❖ ❖ ❖

Lay Down Your Heavy Burdens

Cast your burden upon the Lord, and he will sustain you: he will not suffer the righteous to be moved. Psalm 55:22

There are times when life's struggles make us feel like giving up. We may be going through a season when all seems hopeless. Is there anything we can do to change the condition or circumstances? If we stopped for a moment, prayed and asked God to direct us, we would know to cast all burdens at His feet and leave them there. Through every trial, God is right there in the midst. He gives us strength to walk through every valley.

Worrying about the past and future only brings unnecessary stress. It is time to lay our burdens down. It's time to let go of past mistakes and ask God for forgiveness. God desires that we live life without guilt and shame. Get rid of the attitude of believing the world owes us something. There are no benefits in comparing ourselves to others and what they own. We only create added burdens when trying to live above our income. Unload unnecessary collected baggage and get prepared for what God has designed! It is time to get our joy back. Bow down and worship God. He

45

will lift burdens, give directions, and meet all our needs.

Prayer For Today: Lord as I cast my cares upon you, help me surrender all burdens to you. God keep me from worry and doubt. Strengthen my mind as I walk in your peace, love, grace, and protection. In Jesus name I pray, Amen.

Lay Down Your Heavy Burdens (Day 12)

Scripture: Matthew 11:30, Psalm 118:24

_____

_____

_____

_____

_____

_____

_____

_____

_____

_____

_____

_____

_____

_____

_____

_____

_____

————————— ❖ ❖ ❖ —————————

DAY 13

❖ ❖ ❖

Living In Expectancy

Find rest, O my soul, in God alone; my hope comes from him. Psalm 62:5

According to the dictionary, the word 'expect' means to wait for, to look for as likely to occur or appear, to look forward to, anticipate, to look for as due, proper, or necessary. It implies a considerable degree of confidence that a particular event will happen. When we have prayed and asked God for change, healing, and restoration, we must believe and expect Him to answer.

Jesus said, "If you ask anything in my name, I will do it" (John 14:14). God can and will work out every situation according to His purpose. We expect God to work miracles in our lives. Whatever obstacle is standing in our way, we trust God to change the situation, or change us for the situation. He will either move the mountain or give us strength to move around it.

Attempt the impossible and expect the miraculous. The problems we are agonizing over, the situations weighing heavy on our mind, we give it over to God expecting Him to resolve it. Trust God and expect Him to give us peace. Today we see ourselves refreshed; doing things we have

47

not been able to do in a while. God gives us renewed strength and new life. Expect God to provide in ways as never before. He keeps His promises. Wait on the Lord and be of good courage...and expect great results.

Prayer For Today: Lord please grant me 'now faith' to live in expectancy of all you have planned for me. Guide my thoughts in knowing you will fulfill every promise. I expect to experience miracles, healings, signs, and wonders. Help me to trust and not doubt. In Jesus name I pray, Amen.

Living In Expectancy (Day 13)

Scriptures: Romans 8:28, Ephesians 3:20

_____

_____

_____

_____

_____

_____

_____

_____

_____

_____

_____

_____

❖ ❖ ❖

DAY 14

⋅⊹⋅ ⋅⊹⋅ ⋅⊹⋅

Jesus Knows How To Respond To Our Situation

I called upon the Lord in distress; the Lord answered me and set me in a large place.
Psalm 118:5

You may be saying one of the following, "Lord I need you to fix the mess going on in my life right now. I am at the end of my rope. My children are disobedient; they are going their own way into a life of self-destruction. My marriage is emotionally unbalanced; the love has all faded away. My funds are low, and my rent/mortgage is past due. My car is in need of repair, again. My body is full of pain. I am about to collapse under the pressure. God if you don't intervene, I will not make it."

Hold on, help is on the way! When all hope seems to be fading, God's Word tells us to "Lean not to our own understanding, but in all our ways acknowledge Him, and He will direct our path" (Proverbs 3:5-6). There are many signs and wonders in the New Testament validating the miracles of Jesus. He responded each time with a few powerful words. Jesus boldly declared, "Take up your bed and walk," "Peace be still," "Be healed and go in peace," "Your sins are forgiven." Whatever our circumstances at the moment, Jesus knows, and He will respond. I am a living witness. He always responds to our call for help. Jesus may not always answer the way we think He will, but He is faithful in fulfilling every promise in His time and in His own way.

Prayer For Today: Lord God keep me from giving up while waiting for your response. Give me the faith needed to stand when it looks opposite of what you promised. Keep me strong during difficult seasons. I decree and declare your will is done for my life. In Jesus name I pray, Amen.

Jesus Knows How To Respond To Our Situation (Day 14)

Scriptures: Psalm 30:5, Matthew 9:2, Luke 13:11, John 5:8

_____

_____

_____

_____

_____

_____

_____

_____

——————— ✠ ✠ ✠ ———————

DAY 15

You Have Loved Me

*"The Lord has appeared of old unto me,
saying, Yea, I have loved you with an
everlasting love; therefore with loving
kindness have I drawn you."*
Jeremiah 31:3

I reflect on the days when only hopelessness
was glaring down on my situation. I was in a
state of confusion. My life was filled with despair,
and everything was spiraling downward. I was
hurt, lonely, and sad. Yet God loved me when I
wanted to give up. He was there in the midnight
hour when I had no friend to call on. God was
there all the time, and He continues to love me.
Where would any of us be without the love of God
guiding and supporting us?

The winds and waves of life have tossed us
about and left us bruised, but God is love. At
times, we don't understand all God is doing, but
know His great love never fails. Although we may
feel angry and frustrated for a season, God is
close, and He can see our tears. When it aches in
the pit of our being, God is still upholding and
strengthening us. His love and compassion are
far beyond our comprehension. When we confess
our sin and ask forgiveness, we are forgiven. We

receive God's grace and mercy continually. His mercies are new every morning. His love for us is from everlasting to everlasting.

Prayer For Today: Thank you Lord for healing me spiritually, physically, and emotionally by your divine love. Please give me wisdom, knowledge, and understanding. Continue to strengthen, guide and watch over me. Help me to share your love with others. I love and adore you. In Jesus name I pray, Amen.

You Have Loved Me (Day 15)

Scriptures: 2 Kings 20:5, Psalm 145:9, Hebrews 13:5, I John 4:9

_____

_____

_____

_____

_____

_____

_____

_____

_____

_____

_____

✛ ✛ ✛

DAY 16

⁜ ⁜ ⁜

Getting My 'Self' Out of God's Way

"He that has no rule over his own spirit is like a city that is broken down, without walls." Proverbs 25:28

The self that needs to move out of God's way is self-centered, self-righteous, self-seeking, self-absorbed, and just plain selfish. Why are we vain, arrogant, conceited, overbearing and full of ourselves? No one can tell us anything because we think we are always right. We are self-willed and self-determined to go our own way. We believe we have all the answers. We leave no room for growth, healing, and no room for God to speak. To go a step further, there is also self-hatred, self-doubt, and poor self-esteem.

We wallow in beds we have made for ourselves, not really knowing how to get up. We struggle to stay comfortable in situations in which we have no control. We cry to others for sympathy, but we have created some of these hindrances. Sometimes we find ourselves in despair and full of self-denial. In every instance, 'self' is always getting disappointed. How can we change and become the person God desires? Simply, we must surrender our 'self' over to God and allow Him to mold and reshape us. God has to prune us and cut away the attitudes and behaviors that weigh us down. Make a conscious decision to get 'self' out of the way, so the light of Christ can shine forth and draw others to Him.

Prayer For Today: Lord take full control of my life and order my footsteps. Help me get out of my own way and to stop blocking my blessings. God please keep me from distractions, and keep me from becoming sidetracked. Help me not to abort the plans you have for my life. In Jesus name I pray, Amen.

Getting My 'Self' Out Of God's Way (Day 16)

Scriptures: Hosea 10:12, Matthew 26:41

_____

_____

_____

_____

_____

_____

_____

_____

_____

_____

_____

————————— ❖ ❖ ❖ —————————

DAY 17

✣ ✣ ✣

Be Encouraged

**"The name of the Lord is a strong tower: the
righteous run in and is safe."
Proverbs 18:10**

During times of illness, defeat, discouragement, and depression, I must press through
and receive God's grace. When people talk about
me and slander my name, I will not be moved nor
hang my head down. I will lift up my eyes to the
Lord. My help comes from the Lord, creator of
heaven and earth (Psalm 121:1-2). We speak the
Word of God to encourage ourselves. As we speak
the desired outcome in the will of God, He shall
bring it to pass. Our healing and breakthroughs
are in our mouths. Death and life are in the power
of the tongue. We speak those things that are not
as though they were.

Today, we make declarations such as, "I walk
in victory." "I hold onto the promises of God." "I
am and I remain debt free." "I no longer fear
rejection from others." "I am not weary in well
doing." "I walk in peace, prosperity and divine
health." "I know and always believe Satan is a
defeated foe." "God is for me; No one and nothing
can stand against me." "I am blessed in the city

55

and blessed in the field." "I am the head and not the tail."

Shout to the Lord in the voice of triumph because a new day dawns! A new season, new mercies, and new blessings await!... Be encouraged... Hallelujah!!!!

Prayer For Today: Lord I open my heart to receive your Word. Give me clarity of thought that I may be uplifted and encouraged. Allow your Holy Word to penetrate my mind and heart. I am encouraged to know everything happening in my life is working together for good. I have complete victory in every area. In Jesus name, Amen.

Be Encouraged (Day 17)

Scriptures: 1 Samuel 30:6, Psalm 91:7-11, Philippians 4:13

_____

_____

_____

_____

_____

_____

_____

_____

_____

_____

❖ ❖ ❖

DAY 18

—————— ✤ ✤ ✤ ——————

Be Set Free

*"And at midnight Paul and Silas prayed,
and sang praises unto God: and the
prisoners heard them. And suddenly there
was a great earthquake, so that the
foundations of the prison were shaken: and
immediately all the doors were opened, and
every one's bands were loosed."*
(Acts 16:25-26)

During the course of life, we set up mini
prisons in our minds. Past experiences have
a way of holding us in bondage. Oftentimes,
unflattering memories of childhood keep
replaying over and over. Perhaps, we acted out of
character in our teens or young adult years. Our
prayers for forgiveness and release seemed to
have fallen by the wayside. Guilt and shame hold
us in bondage for a long time and continue to
haunt us.

It is possible to feel bound because of something a family member did, or by our own
thoughts and perception of what actually took
place. Negative beliefs about ourselves can keep
us in unnecessary bondage. One wrong act does
not disqualify us from accomplishing great things
for God. When we seek, pray, and surrender, He

is merciful to forgive us. He still honors our faith. God still desires to use us for His glory. God desires that we live in freedom. We are no longer bound to our past, we have been set free by the love of Christ Jesus. Be reminded, what we did, what we neglected to do, and all our failures and disappointments have already been forgiven. God's grace and mercy follow us all the days of our lives. There is freedom in a Spirit filled life with Christ. We continue to live drama free and stress free. Chains are broken as we walk the path of freedom for the rest of our lives.

Prayer For Today: Lord God please draw me closer to you. Heal me of haunting memories that attempt to hold me in bondage. Set my heart, mind, and spirit free. I desire to walk in your freedom from this day and forever. In Jesus name, Amen.

Be Set Free (Day 18)

Scriptures: Psalm 103:12, John 8:32

_____

_____

_____

_____

_____

_____

_____

———————— ✢ ✢ ✢ ————————

DAY 19

.:. .:. .:.

Be Strong and Very Courageous

Be strong and very courageous. Be careful to obey all the instructions Moses gave you. Do not deviate from them, turning either to the right or to the left. Then you will be successful in everything you do.
(Joshua 1:7)

Do you ever feel like giving up? Ever ask yourself what is this entire God thing all about? Well, if we are not daily seeking God's presence and power, we may sometimes experience doubt. Others will ask us about God and why we believe. The enemy is constantly attacking us on every side. Satan will try to weaken our mind and spirit with questions and fear. His only purpose is to steal, kill, destroy, and block us from reaching our highest potential in Christ.

Today, let us be reminded that whatever we are going through, whether it is a personal health challenge, declining health of a loved one, loss of a loved one, financial difficulty, problems on the job, unemployment, situations in our home or family, or some other emotional frustrations, we are more than conquerors through Him that loved us (Romans 8:37). Pressures of life come to test, change, and strengthen us. No matter how dark the night or how lonely the journey seems, we can trust and lean on the Lord. God is the source of our strength. All of our help comes from Him. Today, be strong and very courageous in the Lord.

Prayer For Today: Lord please give me courage to obey your voice. Show me where to find strength and courage when there seems to be none. Please give me victory through every storm and tribulation. Strengthen me for every test, every battle and every adversity that tries to destroy me or my family. In the name of Jesus, I pray and give thanks, Amen.

Be Strong and Very Courageous (Day 19)

Scriptures: Proverbs 31:17, Isaiah 40:31, Ephesians 6:10

_____

_____

_____

_____

_____

_____

_____

_____

_____

❖ ❖ ❖

DAY 20

❖ ❖ ❖

Clothed In Humility

Clothe yourselves all of you, with humility toward one another, for God opposes the proud but gives grace to the humble.
1 Peter 5:5

There are many expressions of humility all around us. Take a closer look at the men and women God has placed in our paths. There are countless people who have done great things, and no one knew of their accomplishments until we saw the documentaries or read their books. We have certain family members who have made great accomplishments as well. All these men and women had no time to brag about what they were doing. They only knew something had to be done quickly. They were busy executing their plans and projects; not focusing on what others said or thought. They moved in quiet confidence, all the while remaining humble. Sometimes, they sat quietly while others received all the credit.

The truth always comes to light. All who played a role in production will be revealed, and if not, it means God got the glory. It simply means we are important to God and we can be trusted. It is not about us being seen nor having our names called out for recognition. Our time will come, and we will be rewarded by God for our faithfulness. So, be clothed in humility. Do what is required at the right time. Let your good works be seen by others so they can glorify God.

Prayer For Today: Lord please keep me humble and awake to hear your voice of instructions that I may continue to do your will. Let there be no pride and arrogance in me. Keep me from being loud and boastful. Help me walk in the spirit of humility. In Jesus name I pray, Amen.

Clothed In Humility (Day 20)

Scriptures: Proverbs 22:4, Zephaniah 2:3, Colossians 3:12-15, 1 Peter 5:5-6

_____

_____

_____

_____

_____

_____

_____

_____

_____

_____

_____

_____

_____ ❖ ❖ ❖ _____

DAY 21

✠ ✠ ✠

Prosper Where You Are Planted

Beloved, I wish above all things that you may prosper and be in health, even as your soul prospers. 3 John 2

Many are called but few are chosen. Some are called and anointed to be pastors, teachers, or leaders. Many of us may never wear a title, stand in a great cathedral, or be asked to lead a special committee. Yet, God has given each of us an assignment. There are several things we have been gifted and anointed by God to do. We may be asking, "How can I go unless I'm sent?" "How can I be sent unless I'm called?"

God is saying, "I have chosen you, sanctified you, and anointed you to go into places only you can go. You have been planted in your family and home, marriage, relationships, on your job, and in your community for a purpose. Go forth and prosper. The prosperity is not for you, but you will share in the harvest."

God has equipped us to make a difference in the lives of those around us. We are planted to help provide for others; to grow, blossom, point others to Christ, and produce much fruit that will bring about positive change. We will reap what we sow. What kind of seeds are we planting? What fruits are we bearing? Are we approachable for anyone to share a fruit from our spiritual tree? When we are planted to produce much fruit, then a harvest of love, joy, peace, longsuffering, gentleness, goodness, faith, meekness, and temperance is what we can expect.

Prayer For Today: Lord God help me grow and prosper where I have been placed. God help me sow good seeds in good ground for a bountiful and nourishing harvest. Help me to do all things in the spirit of love, peace, and joy. In Jesus name I pray and give thanks, Amen.

Prosper Where You Are Planted (Day 21)

Scriptures: Psalm 1:3, I Corinthians 3:5-6, Galatians 5:22-23

❖ ❖ ❖

DAY 22

✛ ✛ ✛

Know How To Give Thanks

Let the word of Christ dwell in you richly in all wisdom: teaching and admonishing one another in psalms and hymns and spiritual songs, singing with grace in your hearts to the Lord. And whatsoever you do in word or deed, do all in the name of the Lord Jesus, giving thanks to God and the Father by him.
Colossians 3:16

Give thanks to God in all things, for He is the giver of life. Give thanks with a grateful heart. Here are a few suggestions: (1) Give thanks as you are able to give your time and service to a worthy cause, (2) Give thanks as you spend time with your mate, children, loved ones and friends, (3) Give thanks by giving to others in need, (4) Give thanks while listening to a dear friend who is going through a tough, unpleasant situation, and remind him or her of their many past blessings, (5) Give thanks even when temporarily lacking in some areas, for God comes to our rescue in unimaginable ways, (6) Give thanks for every answered prayer, (7) Give thanks, no matter what's going on in life, (8) Give thanks and be grateful to God even when we have not received answers. We cannot successfully make it on our own. We will always need God. We continually seek God's presence in our lives. Lord, we give you reverence, thanking you for all things great and small.

Prayer For Today: Lord God please keep me humble and thankful for your many blessings. Walk with me, guide my footsteps, and lead me into your truth and understanding. I thank you for breath, life, health, family, and love. In Jesus name I pray and give thanks, Amen.

Know How To Give Thanks (Day 22)

Scriptures: Psalm 105:1, Psalm 18:49, Ephesians 5:20, 1 Thessalonians 5:18

_____

_____

_____

_____

_____

_____

_____

_____

_____

_____

_____

_____

⁘ ⁘ ⁘

DAY 23

✢ ✢ ✢

Yes, I Want To Be Made Whole

One of the men lying there had been sick for thirty-eight years. When Jesus saw him and knew he had been ill for a long time, he asked him, "Would you like to get well?"
John 5:5-6

We are created by a living, loving God who formed us whole. Yet life in general and choices we make propel us into different situations that sometime leave us feeling broken and incomplete. Winds and waves of life have left us holding on for dear life itself. We have been battered, torn, betrayed, beaten, and bruised. We have been told we are not good enough. Many of us came from broken families. At some point, we were told we are not smart enough, and our lives will never amount to anything.

Satan has stolen our joy by making us believe our lives are hopeless and will never be meaningful again. The devil is the master of lies. He tries desperately to control our thoughts in order to hold us in fear and bondage. Through it all, we have a hope in Christ Jesus; He still loves us in our brokenness. Jesus loves us into complete and divine health. Only God can wipe away painful memories of our past and bring deliverance. God keeps us. His Word constantly reminds us that we are whole and complete in Him.

Prayer For Today: Dear Lord, I call upon you to heal my hurts, scars, and brokenness and make me whole. Heal the root cause of my suffering, and take away all pains of my past. God renew my strength in you. I give you thanks and praise in Jesus name, Amen.

Yes, I want To Be Made Whole (Day 23)

Scriptures: Mark 10:52, Luke 8:48, Luke 17:18-19

_____

_____

_____

_____

_____

_____

_____

_____

_____

_____

_____

_____

_____

⁙ ⁙ ⁙

DAY 24

‡ ‡ ‡

Wait On The Lord

**Wait on the Lord: be of good courage, and he
shall strengthen thine heart: wait, I say on
the Lord. Psalm 27:14**

We all have seasons where life's pressures
weigh us down. We grow weary, often
wondering if God is even listening to our prayers.
Our faith is in question and no one seems to care.
No answers are coming forth, and God is silent. It
is at this time that we must wait for divine
guidance and put our faith into action. We call
forth those things that are not as though they
already exist.

Here are some things to do while waiting on
the Lord: (1)Wait in Bible Study and reading
God's Word at home, (2) Wait while kneeling to
pray, (3) Wait while being a cheerful giver, (4) Wait
while sharing your testimony and witnessing to
someone about Jesus Christ, (5) Wait while
visiting the elderly, sick and shut-in, (6) Wait
doing errands for the physically challenged, and
(7) Wait while rejoicing over someone else's
breakthrough blessings, knowing ours is on the
way. Continue being blessed by waiting on the
Lord. He is faithful to His Word.

Prayer For Today: Lord give me the patience to wait on you. Instead of being idle, let me be busy about your business and helping build your Kingdom. Help me not to get angry, frustrated, impatient, or doubtful while waiting. Help me to wait patiently on your promises for my life. In Jesus name, Amen.

Wait On The Lord (Day 24)

Scriptures: Psalm 37:7, Isaiah 40:31

_____

_____

_____

_____

_____

_____

_____

_____

_____

_____

_____

_____

_____

❖ ❖ ❖

DAY 25

———————— ⁙ ⁙ ⁙ ————————

I Will Not Be Weary

***And let us not be weary in well doing: for in
due season we shall reap, if we faint not.
Galatians 6:9***

We constantly give our all, and no one calls to
give a word of appreciation. We volunteer,
stay up late at night making preparations, and
give our time to worthy causes. We receive no
recognition for the work we have done or are
currently still doing. We say to ourselves, *"No one
ever appreciates the things I do. I will just stay
home from now on because no one even noticed I
was there."*

We all have moments of feeling inadequate,
unloved, unappreciated, and insignificant. Do not
grow weary when it appears you're the only one
giving, the only one paying for dinner, and never
being treated fairly. Do not become weary if you
are the only sibling taking care of an ailing loved
one, the only one giving a ride to someone without
transportation, the only one staying late to clean
up, the only one making the meals, or the only
one providing a place for the relative who just lost
their home. Don't grow weary when it seems as
though evil is being rewarded and good is being
punished. Always remember God is watching. He

knows our actions and intentions, and He will reward our faithfulness.

Prayer For Today: Lord God give me patience. Help me not to grow weary when helping others. Remind me how you have blessed me to be a blessing. Help me to serve in obedience and love. God please continue to strengthen me as I do your will. In Jesus name, Amen.

I Will Not Become Weary (Day 25)

Scriptures: Isaiah 40:31, Luke 6:38

_____

_____

_____

_____

_____

_____

_____

_____

_____

_____

_____

_____

_____

✛ ✛ ✛

DAY 26

⁘ ⁘ ⁘

Divine Healing

And Jesus went about all the cities and villages, teaching in their synagogues, and preaching the gospel of the kingdom, and healing every sickness and every disease among the people.
Matthew 9:35

The divine healing power of God is needed in every area, physically, spiritually, and psychologically. We have injuries, scars, and life-threatening problems that need His healing touch.

God, please heal our minds. Change our way of thinking. Remove the negative thoughts that hinder us from walking into our divine destiny. Heal our low self-esteem. God, please heal our body. Heal all cancer, diabetes, high and low blood pressure, arthritis, multiple sclerosis, hepatitis, AIDS, sickle cell anemia, stomach ailments, joint disease, tumors, insomnia, and all other ailments. God, please heal us from abuse. Heal us from memories of molestation, spousal abuse, parental abuse, and child abuse. God, please heal our spirit. Free us from demonic oppression. Deliver us from the spirit of gambling, fornication, lust, lying, deception, drugs, and alcohol. Deliver us from jealousy and pride.

Prayer For Today: Dear Lord, you are The Great Physician. I lay these and all petitions on the altar asking that you would heal every area of my life. O God, I stand on your Word that you will perfect that which concerns me. By your stripes I am already healed. Thank you for divine healing already taking place. In Jesus name I pray, Amen.

Divine Healing (Day 26)

Scriptures: Isaiah 53:5, Psalms 6:2, Jeremiah 30:17, Psalms 30:2

_____

_____

_____

_____

_____

_____

_____

_____

_____

_____

❖ ❖ ❖

DAY 27

◆ ◆ ◆

I Have The Victory

For whatsoever is born of God overcomes the world: and this is the victory that overcomes the world, even our faith. Who is he that overcomes the world, but he that believes that Jesus is the Son of God? (1 John 5:4-5)

We have victory over every barrier and obstacle that comes our way. God has promised never to leave nor forsake us. Things may seem uncertain, but God has promised to supply all of our needs. Personally speaking, I've experienced some painful setbacks. My life felt like a bottomless pit. Satan came in like a roaring lion to devour me, but God stepped in and gave me victory. I prayed daily and meditated on Scriptures. My enemies did not triumph over me. "No weapon formed against me shall prosper; and every lying tongue that shall rise against me in judgement you shall condemn..." (Isaiah 54:17).

Challenging situations still arise but I have the peace of God, which passes all understanding. I will not be defeated. I surrender myself to God and walk in total obedience. I pray without ceasing. My plate is turned down as I fast seeking God. I hold onto my faith believing victory is mine.

Prayer For Today: Lord please keep me from giving up and sinking into despair. Remind me of your steadfast love. With your help I can stand strong in faith. Thank you for making ways when there seemed to be only obstacles. Thank you for making me an overcomer and empowering me to walk in victory. In Jesus name, Amen.

I Have The Victory (Day 27)

Scriptures: Ephesians 6:10-13, Philippians 4:13

_____

_____

_____

_____

_____

_____

_____

_____

_____

_____

_____

_____

_____

❖ ❖ ❖

DAY 28

✤ ✤ ✤

Salt And Light

You are the salt of the earth, but if the salt loses its flavor, how shall it be seasoned? It is then good for nothing but to be thrown out and trampled underfoot by men. You are the light of the world. A city that is set on a hill cannot be hidden. Nor do they light a lamp and put it under a basket, but on a lampstand, and it gives light to all who are in the house. Let your light so shine before men, that they may see your good works and glorify your Father in heaven.
Matthew 5:13-16

The minute we leave home, we are being watched by someone. Unsuspectingly, we are being closely examined. Our walk with Christ is always in the spotlight. When others look at us, they should see something that's different and unique. Our relationship with God is recognizable to many who are discerning. Our actions do speak louder than our words. We cannot forget who we are in Christ. We are new creations, and former things have passed away.

Here are some questions to ponder: (1) Am I sharing the Word of God, or am I hiding my kinship and love for Jesus Christ? (2) Can those around me see and say there's something different about me? and (3) Do others seek me out for prayer, godly counsel, and encouragement when they face difficulties or have a need? There is an aura about those who spend time with God. Our light shines when we enter dark places. The atmosphere changes when we enter a room. Remember God has equipped us to be salt and light...to make a difference in the lives of others.

Prayer For Today: Lord please help me walk in wisdom as I continue to be salt and light. Let those around me see and feel your love through my actions. Help me God to share peace, love, and joy along life's journey. Let your light shine in and through me. In Jesus name I pray, Amen.

Salt and Light (28)

Scripture: Colossians 4:5-6

_____
_____
_____
_____
_____
_____
_____
_____
_____

⊹ ⊹ ⊹

DAY 29

❖ ❖ ❖

These Bones Can Live

The hand of the Lord came upon me and brought me out in the Spirit of the LORD, and set me down in the midst of the valley, and it was full of bones. Then He caused me to pass by them all around, and behold, there were very many in the open valley, and indeed they were very dry. And He said to me, "Son of man, can these bones live?" So I answered, "O Lord, You know."
Ezekiel 37:1-3

Has life ever hit you so hard that you asked the following questions, "Lord will I make it through this storm?" "When will this sickness leave my body?" "Will I ever get well?" When we face problems that seem impossible to solve, the spiritual question that comes to mind is, *"Can these bones live?"*

Here are some examples of 'dry bones' experiences in life: (1) Living with anger and unforgiveness; (2) Being worn down and tired from the cares of everyday life; (3) Going through difficult times on your job; (4) Endless marital problems; (5) Children gone astray; (6) Struggling in deep financial debt; (7) Battling a drug, alcohol or sexual addiction; and there are many others. A great majority of us, at one time or another, have been through a valley of dry bones experiences. But the good news is God is still healing, delivering, restoring, blessing, and performing miracles. No matter how dark the night, we are reminded Jesus loves us and joy does come in the morning. Yes, these bones can live. Hallelujah!

Prayer For Today: Lord please continue to heal and restore me spiritually, physically, and mentally. Strengthen me so that my bones can live. Cover me and set me on a straight path to continual victory. Order my footsteps in your will dear God. I worship you always. It's in you that I live and have my being. In Jesus name I pray, Amen.

Can These Bones Live (Day 29)

Scriptures: Ezekiel 37:4-7, John 10:10

_____

_____

_____

_____

_____

_____

_____

_____

_____

Peace by The River

A walk, a rest by the water's edge
Inquisitive geese perched on their nesting ledge
Soft breezes caress my face
No other place
I'd ever dare to embrace,
To catch a memory of you
A glimpse or echo of things you'd do.
The water, the sounds beckon me near
Your voice, again I'd love to hear
Far from the shore you've gone
To your heavenly eternal resting home
Way past yonder,
My spirit and mind wander
What appeared impossible many days
You made clear in so many ways.
I have no fear,
It's your voice I hear
When I draw near
My path's made clear
Oh yes, I give thanks
On the gentle riverbanks!

By Katherine L. Harvell

———— ✥ ✥ ✥ ————

Be careful for nothing; but in every thing by prayer and supplication with thanksgiving let your requests be made known unto God. And the peace of God, which passeth all understanding, shall keep your hearts and minds through Christ Jesus.
Philippians 4:6-7

———— ✥ ✥ ✥ ————

DAY 30

❖ ❖ ❖

A New Way of Thinking

**Behold, the former things are come to pass.
And the new things do I declare: before they
spring forth I tell you of them.
Isaiah 42:9**

Our minds have been cleared of some things, and we have a new way of thinking. Whatever happened in the past is staying in the past. We cannot look at things the same old way and expect change to occur. God has enabled us to see situations differently, and we have a new way of understanding. Our minds are clear for new vision, new opportunities, and new relationships. The light has been turned on. We step out with boldness knowing God is with us now and always has been. We are able to stand unashamedly, declaring the goodness of the Lord and all He is doing in our lives. We are forgetting about the things behind and pressing forward to the things God has already prepared. Therefore, we are able to be a blessing to others.

God is always on the scene working things out in our affairs. In all things, God works for the good of those who love him, who are the called according to his purpose (Romans 8:28).

Prayer For Today: Lord heal my mind, and give me clarity of thought. Enable me to think on things that are honorable and pleasing to you. I praise you God for new mercies and new insight. Glory and honor belong to you. I give thanks for all things are working together for the good. In Jesus name I pray, Amen.

A New Way of Thinking (30)

Scriptures: Isaiah 43:19, Philippians 4:8

_____

_____

_____

_____

_____

_____

_____

_____

_____

_____

_____

_____

_____

❖ ❖ ❖

DAY 31

⁜ ⁜ ⁜

The Anointing

Then the men of David said to him, "This is the day of which the Lord said to you, 'Behold, I will deliver the enemy into your hand, that you may do to him as it seems good to you.' " And David arose and secretly cut off a corner of Saul's robe. Now it happened afterward that David's heart troubled him because he had cut Saul's robe. And he said to his men, "The Lord forbid that I should do this thing to my master, the Lord's anointed, to stretch out my hand against him, seeing he is the anointed of the Lord." 1 Samuel 24:4-6

The anointing of God is upon us, and we have been chosen to follow in the ministry of Jesus Christ preaching, teaching, and praying for the sick. God desires us to have clean hands and a pure heart, so His anointing can flow freely through us to help bless others. The anointing causes us to seek the will of God. He causes us to give our resources, our time, and our services. The anointing requires our trust in God. Jesus Christ paid the ultimate price so that the anointing of God could dwell within us. What a sacrifice He made for us all. Beginning today, place all concerns on the altar. Pick up the cross and follow Christ. The anointing cost too much. We cannot afford to dishonor God. Be obedient to the anointing God has placed inside of all blood washed believers.

Prayer For Today: Lord I humbly ask you to anoint me afresh and renew a right spirit within me. Cleanse me of everything contrary to your will for my life. Revive, refresh, restore, and make me whole. Fill me with a fresh wind of your Holy Spirit. In Jesus name, Amen.

The Anointing (Day 31)

Scriptures: 1 John 2:27, I Corinthians 6:20

_____

_____

_____

_____

_____

_____

_____

_____

_____

_____

_____

_____

⁜ ⁜ ⁜

DAY 32

⁘ ⁘ ⁘

God's Loving Grace

And He said unto me, "My grace is sufficient for thee: for my strength is made perfect in weakness. Most gladly therefore will I rather glory in my infirmities, that the power of Christ may rest upon me. 2 Corinthians 12:9

Grace is favor or kindness shown without regard to a person's worth or merit. Grace is given regardless of whether we think we deserve it or not. It is one of the key attributes of God. Grace is associated with mercy, love, compassion, and patience. We are all recipients of God's loving grace. Take a moment to think about what life would be like right now, had it not been for grace. Grace shields and protects us in our everyday activities. When all else fails, grace is there to pick us up again. Grace is peace, comfort, and strength to go forward; no matter what trials and difficulties we face.

Credit card and loan companies give us grace periods; a few extra days to make payments. God's grace period never depends upon our ability to pay. Whenever we cry out to God for help. He gives us grace. Can we fully recognize the grace of God in our lives? What He has done for us and countless others, He can and will do for others if only they ask. I thank God for second, third, fourth, and many countless chances. Let us remember to give God thanks for grace as He wakes us up each day. We give thanks for grace that shields and protects.

Prayer For Today: Thank you God for grace and mercy each new day. Your grace is my sufficiency. As I strive to do your will Lord, please continue to cover me in your grace, love, favor, and protection. In Jesus name I pray, Amen.

God's Loving Grace (Day 32)

Scriptures: Romans 6:14, I Corinthians 15:10, Ephesians 2:8-9, 4:7, Titus 3:7

_____

_____

_____

_____

_____

_____

_____

_____

_____

_____

_____

⁜ ⁜ ⁜

DAY 33

Being Pruned By God

**Every branch in me that does not bear fruit
he takes away: and every branch that bears
fruit, he purges it, that it may bring forth
more fruit. John 15:2**

Farmers and gardeners cultivate beautiful,
thriving flowers and vegetables. Watering,
fertilizing, spraying, and pruning are continuously
required. We break off the dried, withered leaves
and branches expecting new healthy growth. We
cut off old blooms while expecting new ones to
soon open in their place. Sometimes, we must
uproot our plants and replant them in a different
location. Some roots are stubborn, and weeds
keep growing back. Deeper and larger spaces are
needed for some roots to spread out and flourish.
If we do not prune and snip off the dead branches,
the bad stems will rot the entire plant.

Our lives are much the same as plants. We
need special attention including feeding, watering
and pruning. When left unattended, bitterness
and resentment take hold on the inside causing
our hearts to become stony. God has to dig up
embedded roots of unforgiveness and jealousy.
He has to cut off our complaining, nagging and
prideful attitudes. Just as plants need a fence

around them, sometimes God will put a fence of protection around us for our own good. He shields us from things that are harmful during the pruning process. We have reason to rejoice when God trims off the useless and unnecessary things from our lives. Hallelujah! We are being pruned by God. New growth and new opportunities spring forth with God's special care.

Prayer For Today: Lord God please purge me of every unclean thing. Prune me, and cut off every ungodly, unhealthy habit and thought. I desire to be more like Christ. In Jesus name, Amen.

Being Pruned By God (Day 33)

Scripture: John 15:5-6

_____

_____

_____

_____

_____

_____

_____

_____

_____

_____

_____

_____

⁘ ⁘ ⁘

DAY 34

❖ ❖ ❖

Rest, Remember, Rejoice

**Come to Me, all you who labor and are heavy
laden, and I will give you rest.
Matthew 11:28**

Difficulties arise unexpectedly, and we suddenly become overshadowed by chaos. There is no rest for the weary. It's easy to become entangled with challenges and struggles relating to our spouses, children, or other family members. Our brains are in overdrive, searching for something to say or do to make the situation better. While trying to fix it, we realize God has already worked it out for everyone involved.

Oftentimes, it helps to get away from people, because we are hearing too many voices. It becomes necessary to take time to rest, relax, pray, and listen for the voice of God to direct our path. It also helps to find a quiet place to close our eyes and take some deep breaths. From the moment we decide to rest and give our problems completely over to God, we have assurance that everything is already alright. As we rest, we can remember and give thanks for all the struggles God brought us through. Remember when those bills came; we had no idea how they would get paid. God stepped in right on time. Many times, life knocked us down for the count, but God raised us back up. We rejoice for our relationship with Jesus Christ. When we rest and remember, we have cause to rejoice for what the Lord has brought us through. Therefore, we will rest, remember, and rejoice...and be glad in it. Hallelujah!!

Prayer For Today: Lord Jesus please give me an allotted time to come aside for resting and replenishing. Help me to stay calm no matter the situation. Keep me from becoming weary. God let me rest, remember, rejoice, and continue to give thanks. In Jesus name, Amen.

Rest, Remember, Rejoice (Day 34)

Scriptures: Hebrews 4:3 Psalm 105:5, Psalm 118:24

_____

_____

_____

_____

_____

_____

_____

_____

_____

⁘ ⁘ ⁘

DAY 35

❖ ❖ ❖

What Are You Saying?

Death and life are in the power of the tongue: and they that love it shall eat the fruit thereof. Proverbs 18:21

The Bible tells us our words have power, yet we still make statements such as, "Nothing good ever happens to me." or "I can't do that because I'm too old or too young." Negative statements will keep us in bondage. Are we speaking hope to what seems hopeless? Are we speaking words of healing? Are we speaking those things that are not as though they were? Guarding our tongue is necessary, because the very things we speak have a way of showing up in our own lives. Be consistent in speaking positive things. Having a positive attitude while going through pain will enable us to move into our purpose.

Our words are prayers; so let us be cautious of what we say. Jesus didn't say a lot. His actions spoke louder than His words. He spoke to the lame, and they began to walk. He spoke to blinded eyes and commanded them to see. Jesus' words were always powerful and uplifting. Today, God speaks powerful and uplifting words for our healing. He said, "You are fearfully and wonderfully made." "You are the head and not the tail." and "You shall live and not die." Let us speak life to encourage ourselves. Before we make disempowering declarations about ourselves and others, let's ask the questions, "What would God say? What does His Word say?" He reminds us our words do have power. Let us continue to speak life and uplift ourselves and others.

Prayer For Today: Lord I pray asking you to guard my tongue. Enable me to stay in faith, speaking positive words over my life as well as others. Purify my mind that my heart will speak words of praise and adoration to you God. Give me the right words and enable me to speak them at the proper time. In Jesus name, Amen.

What Are You Saying? (Day 35)

Scripture: Proverbs 18:21

_____

_____

_____

_____

_____

_____

_____

_____

_____

❖ ❖ ❖

DAY 36

While God Is Working On Me

***Being confident of this very thing, that He
who has begun a good work in you will
complete it until the day of Jesus Christ.
Philippians 1:6***

Sometimes we may say the wrong thing, do the
wrong thing, and walk the wrong way.
Sometimes we may stumble, make mistakes, or
have a pity party, but God is there to help. Upon
realizing we have made a mistake, apologize and
repent. Prayer will help us not to be so hard on
ourselves. The key is, do not stay down.
Spectators are always watching to see what we do
when we fall. How do we handle it when others
are talking about us, whispering about our
situation? It is very simple; do not feed into the
negativity of others anymore.

God already knows we are not perfect.
Everyone makes mistakes. He knows our faults
and therefore; He is continuously healing,
molding, and renewing our mind. The negative
comments no longer hurt because we have grown
stronger. We are rejoicing while God is making us
better. Most often a spiritual makeover is painful
because God gets into areas we have been
avoiding. He brings light to the dark areas so we

can be cleansed and set free. We are excited seeing ourselves being renewed. Our character changes. We do not act and talk the same. Day by day, we are a new creation. A lot of things no longer bother us. We have a new attitude and outlook on life. Our lives are forever changed, and God's love is being revealed through our actions. Hallelujah!

Prayer For Today: Lord God please continue working in my life. Heal me and save me, even from myself. Break old habits and unhealthy desires from my life. I desire to obey and follow all things according to your plan and purpose. In Jesus name, Amen.

While God Is Working On Me (Day 36)

Scriptures: Psalm 51:7, II Timothy 2:21, Romans 12:2

_____

_____

_____

_____

_____

_____

_____

_____

_____

_____

⋯ ⋯ ⋯

DAY 37

—————— ✤ ✤ ✤ ——————

In Twenty-One Days

***Then he said, "Do not fear, Daniel, for from
the first day that you set your heart to
understand, and to humble yourself before
your God, your words were heard, and I have
come because of your words. But the prince
of the kingdom of Persia withstood me
twenty-one days; and behold, Michael, one of
the chief princes, came to help me for I had
been left alone there with the kings of
Persia. Daniel 10:12-13***

God said, "I am giving you back everything the
enemy tried to steal from you." Blessings will
overtake us and our families. It's going to rain
down like thunder. The enemy will be turned
back, and every attempt will be thwarted. Doors
that have been closed will open suddenly. Money
that has been held back will be restored within
twenty-one days. Job applications will be favored.
Missing and wayward children will be returned
with God's anointing and understanding. Sickness in our body will be healed. Marriages,
relationships, and friendships will be renewed.
There will be favor on all of our projects. God will
heal everything concerning us. Claim it because
it is already done in the spirit, now it will be

manifested in the natural. God will use us to be a blessing to many. Because of our faithfulness, we will be called out among thousands to receive blessings.

God has seen our tears, He knows our heart, and He has heard our prayers. Within twenty-one days, we can expect God to show up in our situation. He is not a God that goes back on His promises. His Word is true and everlasting, and it shall not return to Him void. His Word will accomplish whatever He sends it to do. We believe; therefore, it shall come to pass.

Prayer For Today: Father, I thank you that you hear and answer my prayers. Thank you in advance for the manifestation of my petitions for myself and my loved ones. Lord grant me vision and discernment to recognize and understand the different ways you are answering my prayers. I give thanks in Jesus name, Amen.

In Twenty-One Days (Day 37)

Scripture: Isaiah 44:3-4

_____

_____

_____

_____

_____

_____

⁜ ⁜ ⁜

DAY 38

⁙ ⁙ ⁙

It's All For My Good

**And we know that all things work together
for good to those who love God, to those who
are the called according to His purpose.
Romans 8:28**

Our minds race, one thought after the other.
"Now that I have this completed, they're
going to do this next. If he said that, next he will
ask for more. If she said that, next she will do
something different." How will we get through the
struggles? Only God knows the mind and heart of
man. Only God can control the outcome. However
life unfolds, it comes down to what's best for
everyone. It is not meant for us to figure it all out.
His ways are way beyond our comprehension. We
can let go and allow God to do what is required
for our healing and deliverance. Only when we
completely surrender and trust God, will we
receive answers to our petitions.

The things happening around us and in our
lives are working for good and for God's glory. If
we have prayed for God to move a particular way
and He moves in a completely different way, it is
meant to be God's way and not ours. It is the will
of God concerning us, and the trials are meant to
strengthen and heal us in all areas. God has not

abandoned us; He wants us to become mature Christians lacking nothing. He desires that we be equipped to minister to others. Let us begin trusting and depending on the one and only Jesus Christ, the one who meant it all for our good! Amen!

Prayer For Today: Dear Lord, please help me remember when I don't understand that all things are working for my good. When things seem unbearable, help me Lord to look to you, the author and finisher of my faith. Hide me in your secret place. Protect me from the storms and snares of the wicked. Surround me with your peace. In Jesus name, Amen.

It's All For My Good (Day 38)

Scripture: James 1:2-3

_____

_____

_____

_____

_____

_____

_____

_____

_____

_____

⸭ ⸭ ⸭

Visions and Dreams

Visions and Dreams
What do they mean?
Where do they come from?
Unseen-seen, clear-cloudy, places-faces,
they go and come.
From childhood til now
some still rest upon my brow.

Visions and Dreams
flow like streams
giving hope and ways to cope.

Visions and Dreams
will unfold, life and reality destined to be told.
The world is waiting for our dreams to take flight,
With God, we walk in His light.
Don't give up, don't lose hope, don't stop.
Keep dreaming, keep praying,
you will reach the top.
It's all in God's time, not yours, theirs, nor mine.
Dreams do come true.
Ultimately, it's all up to God and you!
Write the vision, give it a name,
nurture it and step into your fame.
In God, pray, trust and abide,
He'll never ever leave your side.
Don't give up on your visions,
dreams and hopes.
There may be mountains, valleys, even slopes.
Yet, I'm living proof, there is a reason,
and it'll all come to pass in due season!

Visions and Dreams
Yes, there's much more to them than it seems.
It may take time and appear impossible but
with God we know all things are possible
He holds our revelation and answer to
every situation, every vision and every dream!
Yes, they are real, **Visions and Dreams!**

By Katherine Harvell, 5/3/2019

—————— ⬧ ⬧ ⬧ ——————

*The world is waiting for our dreams
to take flight, With God, we walk in
His light. Don't give up, don't lose
hope, don't stop. Keep dreaming,
keep praying, you will reach the top.*

—————— ⬧ ⬧ ⬧ ——————

DAY 39

— ❖ ❖ ❖ —

Get Your Dream Back

"Here comes the dreamer!" they said to each other. Genesis 37:19

Joseph told his dreams to his brothers and subsequently experienced many setbacks. All along, he was being set up for one of the greatest comeback blessings of his life and for his people. The miracle usually occurs after we've gone through a season of failures. Did we start a business venture, ministry or marriage and it failed? Perhaps the funds flowed differently, or not as quickly as we imagined.

During times of great frustration, we don't know where to turn for help. Oftentimes, we go around crying, complaining, and talking about giving up on our dreams. We question God, "Did I really hear you correctly in telling me to step out and start this venture, did you really tell me to move, did you really tell me to change jobs, and did you really tell me to marry this person?"

During difficult times of uncertainty and when provisions are low, we must pray and lean on God. He promised to never leave us nor forsake us. We still have to trust Him; even when we can't see any trace of Him moving on our behalf. In actuality, many have been set up to receive God's best when least expected. There is no failure, unless we refuse to keep trying. We step back, rest for a season to regain our focus and momentum.

God is standing by watching our faith to see if we really trust Him to bring the dream to life. Previous failures cause us to doubt ourselves and others. Learn the lessons the past taught, then get back up and try again. Maybe the vision was for an appointed time, another season like now. Expectation will cause us to believe God for a more positive outcome this time around. A fresh wind is needed to set sail and get started again. Our dreams are exciting, and they will come to fruition as we stay focused in faith. Keep pressing forward. God has given us these dreams, and He desires to see them fulfilled. God's prosperity awaits us! Get your dreams back! Go for it! Much success awaits us this time around! Be blessed!

Prayer For Today: Lord my dreams seem so far out of my grasp. Help me believe in the ability you've given me. Give me courage to hold onto the dreams. Help me and show me what's required for my success. Open the doors of opportunity, remove stumbling blocks, and help me walk in my true purpose. In Jesus name I pray, Amen.

Get Your Dream Back (Day 39)

Scripture: 3 John 2

_____

_____

_____

_____

_____

_____

_____

_____

_____

_____

_____

_____

_____

_____

_____

_____

❖ ❖ ❖

———— ⚜ ⚜ ⚜ ————

*God is standing by watching our faith
to see if we really trust Him to bring
the dream to life.*

———— ⚜ ⚜ ⚜ ————

DAY 40

❖ ❖ ❖

The Peace of God

You will keep him in perfect peace, whose mind is stayed on You, because he trusts in You. Isaiah 26:3

We search for God's peace when we are confronted with negative situations. Our emotions cause us to feel stressed and helpless. In these moments, we realize our own cares and concerns of others have left us drained. What happens when no peace can be found? Oftentimes, we have prayed and fasted, and yet God is silent. The people around us are still treating us unfairly, all the while asking us to pray for them. What can we do now, God? Where is your peace? The answer is, keep praying and standing on God's Word no matter what comes our way. Not moving ahead of God, we wait patiently for His timing. As we proclaim, "Peace of the Lord be with you," we are speaking a powerful prophetic blessing over the person and everything connected to them.

Everything we need is wrapped in God's peace. In His peace we experience joy, grace, love, healing, deliverance, forgiveness, prosperity, and salvation. Peace is always available to us when we give our cares to the Lord. We are victorious by

107

remembering and following these five truths: 1) God loves us with an everlasting love, 2) We are to be anxious for nothing as we wait on God, 3) In God's peace, there is safety and security, 4) God's peace surpasses all understanding, and 5) God's peace is perfect.

Prayer For Today: Lord God, please continue to give me peace of mind in every situation of my life. Grant peace in my home over my family. Perfect all that concerns me. Guard my thoughts and give me clear vision, revelation, and understanding. Lord, enable me to walk out the rest of my days in your peace. Thank you for keeping me in perfect peace. In Jesus name, Amen.

The Peace of God (Day 40)

Scripture: Psalm 4:8, Philippians 4:6-7

_____

_____

_____

_____

_____

_____

_____

_____

_____

_____

_____

❖ ❖ ❖

Notes

Notes

Notes

Notes

Notes

Notes

Notes

Notes

ABOUT THE AUTHOR

Katherine L. Harvell began her Christian walk with God at the age of five. By age six, she was Holy Spirit filled and enjoying a Pentecostal fellowship right beside her mother. She enjoyed singing with the choir, prayer, and testimony services. Katherine grew up in a rural Southern town in Virginia and is the youngest of nine children.

In her late teens, Katherine moved to New York to live with her sister. She began her career in government working for the Veterans Administration. She transferred and later retired from the United States Postal Service.

Katherine received an Associate of Arts, Liberal Arts and Social Science Specialization and studied Theology at Cathedral Bible Institute in Perth Amboy, New Jersey.

Katherine was married for thirty years to the late Anthony Harvell. She enjoys spending time with her daughter Stephanie, son-in-law Kenneth, granddaughter Simone, and other family and friends.

Katherine became a licensed minister in 2008 by the leadership of Bishop Donald Hilliard, Jr. In 2012, she was ordained Elder by Apostle Lawrence Campbell. Katherine serves in many areas inside the church and in the community. She served in many ministries: hospitality, greeter, choir, Sunday School Teacher, Prison ministry, GriefShare facilitator, and Hospice Volunteer. She served as board member for

United Way, Danville Virginia Rotary Club and currently Virginia Fair Housing.

Katherine loves to travel locally and abroad. Her favorite trip to date is Jerusalem, where she walked in the footsteps of Jesus and was baptized in the Jordan River. Her desire to do evangelical ministry led her to create and host a weekly radio show entitled Sisters Standing 4 Sisters. Her mission is to inspire, uplift, and encourage others in the Lord.

In addition to *"40 Days of Spiritual Crumbs"* Katherine is also the author of *"The Power of Tears"* which can be purchased on Amazon.

You can follow Katherine on Facebook, Instagram, WKBY 1080AM, and Podbean Blog

Facebook: Katherine L. Harvell, Power of Tears, Sisters Standing 4 Sisters

Instagram: @Kathylavonne

WKBY: Sisters Standing 4 Sisters

Podbean Blog: Katherine Harvell's Inspiration

✤ ✤ ✤

ORDER INFORMATION

You can order additional copies of *40 Days of Spiritual Crumbs* by contacting the author directly using the information below.

Contact information:
Katherine L Harvell
P.O. Box 11133
Danville, Virginia 24543

Harvellkatherine.kh@gmail.com
Facebook – Sisters Standing 4 Sisters
Facebook – Katherine L. Harvell
Facebook – The Power of Tears

Books are available at Amazon.com, BN.com
Kindle and Your Local Bookstores (By Request)

———————— ⁘ ⁘ ⁘ ————————

Please leave a review for this book on Amazon and let other readers know how much you enjoyed reading it.

Thank you!

* 9 7 8 1 7 3 3 1 3 5 3 6 8 *